KU-863-057

First published in 1991 by Firefly Books Limited.

This edition published in 1993 by Wayland (Publishers) Ltd.

This revised edition published in 2009 by Wayland,
338 Euston Road, London NW1 3BH.

Wayland Australia
Level 17/207 Kent Street, Sydney, NSW 2000

Consultant: Jane Battell

British Library Cataloguing in Publication Data
Suhr, Mandy
I am growing.–(I'm alive)
1. Human growth–Pictorial works–Juvenile literature.
2. Growth–Pictorial works–Juvenile literature.
I. Title II. Series III. Gordon, Mike.
612.6-dc22

ISBN 9780750259507

Printed in China

Wayland is a division of Hachette Children's Books,
an Hachette UK company.

www.hachette.co.uk

I Am Growing

Written by Mandy Suhr
Illustrated by Mike Gordon

WAYLAND

When I was born I was tiny.
Everyone looked enormous!
But as the weeks went by...

I grew bigger.

I grew heavier.

I learned to crawl...

and then walk.

I learned to talk...

DOG!

and paint.

I learned to write...

and read.

This all happened
as I grew older.

Growing is a funny thing. It seems
to happen without you noticing.

But you are growing all the time.

My mum and dad say I need lots of things to make me grow.

Milk helps to make my teeth and bones strong.

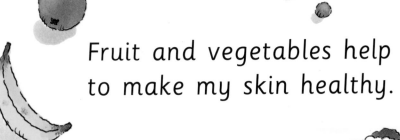

Fruit and vegetables help
to make my skin healthy.

Bread and beans, meat and
fish, eggs and cheese, help to
make my muscles strong.

I need lots of exercise so that my body will grow strong and healthy.

I also need to get plenty of sleep
because growing can be very tiring.

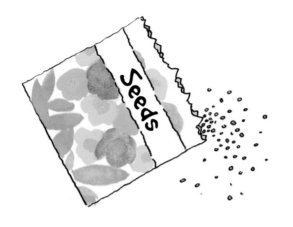

Plants grow, too.
I planted a tiny seed
just like this and now
it's grown into a plant.

Plants need...

food from the soil...

sunshine...

and water...

to make them grow.

Animals grow from little babies just like we do. My cat has had six kittens.

Soon they will grow big
enough to go outside.

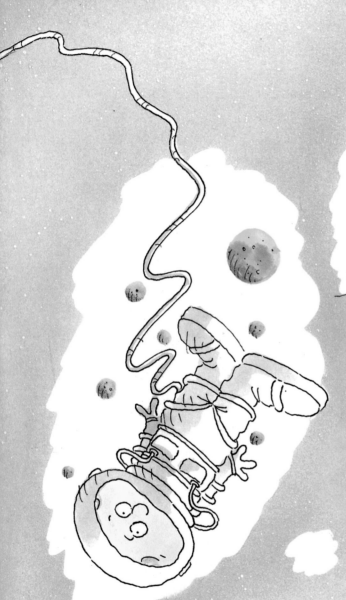

I wonder what I will
be when I grow up?

20

Can you guess what these
babies will grow into?

Notes for Adults

I'm Alive is a series of first information books particularly suitable for the early and emergent stages of reading.

Each book in the series includes simple, factual text, and amusing and colourful illustrations, to combine reading for pleasure with fact-finding.

The series takes a closer look at the human body and how it works and develops, comparing this with other forms of life. **I'm Alive** is designed to address the requirements of the National Curriculum for Science key stage 1.

The books are equally suitable for use at school or at home.
Below are some suggestions for extension activities that can be carried out with children to complement and extend the learning in this book.

Extension Activities

1 Make a 'Baby Book'. Find out about what you were like when you were a baby. Collect photographs and draw pictures. How have you changed over the years?

2 Collect information about the human body and make a poster. Find out how many teeth children and adults have. How many bones are there in the human body? Name different parts of the body.

3 Grow cress seeds and broad beans. Experiment with growing plants in sunny and dark areas. Which is best?

4 Visit a wildlife park, farm or zoo. See how many baby animals you can spot. Look at the differences between the adults and the babies. How have they changed?